The Mystery of

FIRST FRUIT
Offering

DR. D. K. OLUKOYA

THE MYSTERY OF FIRST FRUIT OFFERING

Dr. D. K. Olukoya

The Mystery Of First Fruit Offering
© 2007 *Dr. D. K. Olukoya*
ISBN: **978-0692539064**
Printing - November 2007

Published by:
The Battle Cry Christian Ministries
322, Herbert Macaulay Street, Sabo, Yaba, Lagos.
Phone: 0803-304-4239, 0803-306-0073

All scriptures quotations are from the King James version of the Bible.

Cover illustration: Pastor (Mrs.) Shade Olukoya

TABLE OF CONTENTS

The Mystery Of First Fruit Offering

Prosperity or wealth has secrets. The richest are not necessarily those who sweat ceaselessly night and day. There are lots of people, all over the world, who have stumbled upon the mystery of prosperity. Such people have been catapulted to greatness and taken to unusual heights in the area of prosperity.

The secrets of prosperity have brought untold benefits to the lives of multitudes all over the world. When God gives you access to the mystery of prosperity you will suddenly find yourself surrounded and enveloped by what can be termed dominion prosperity. As far as divine prosperity is concerned, there are certain keys that God has kept for those He wants to let into its secrets.

THE KEY TO PROSPERITY
Prosperity is the exclusive preserve of God. One of the names of God is Jehovah Jireh. This divine attribute portrays Him as the great provider, in whose storehouse there are inexhaustible riches. When you have an encounter with Jehovah Jireh you have come across the God who gives again and again until you experience an overflow. The God whom we serve trades in abundance. He has more than enough resources to bless His children. However, prosperity is not meant for those who are not willing to follow divine principles, but for those who obey them.

Prosperity is as simple as a, b, c. One of the paradoxes of life is that the greatest achievements in life are not necessarily struggled for. The key to the greatest house of treasure is not necessarily the most gigantic of all keys. When God wants to prosper you He will simplify situations around you. Just one step taken in the right direction will lead you into the doors of breakthroughs, which will leave you wealthy for the rest of your life.

THE PRINCIPLES

This book unveils the mystery of prosperity. A careful application of its principles will place the keys of prosperity in your hands. You will be launched into the depths of an ocean of wealth which never dries. The Bible has a lot to say concerning the mystery of first fruit offering. To understand this mystery you need to be reminded of the fact that a powerful prophecy has been given by God concerning the members of Mountain of Fire and Miracles World-wide. God has declared that the they will be the richest and most prosperous of all believers all over the world.

Please, take note of the following facts:

There are 13 major keys provided by God to launch His people into uncommon prosperity. Each key will throw the doors of prosperity wide open. However, some of them are more powerful than the others. Again, some of them have functions that differ slightly from the others. However, an understanding of them will arm you with what it takes to experience and enjoy lasting divine prosperity.

Key No. 1

Make God your friend: The blessings of God are meant for His friends. God is under no obligation to bless His enemies. Friends of God are those who obey His word and do His will. God has no business with wasting his precious resources on those who are one leg in the world and another in the church. When you make God your friend you position yourself where you can receive His blessings. The Scriptures rings out a note of clarity. It declares, "Say ye to the wicked, it shall be ill with him". Remember, anyone who is living in any known sin is an enemy of God. When you live righteously and walk uprightly you will rise up with boldness to possess your possessions in the area of wealth.

Key No. 2

Seek God's kingdom: The Bible says, "Seek ye first the kingdom of God and His righteousness and all other things shall be added unto you. "You must set your priority right. You must give prominence to God's kingdom before giving any consideration to earthly concerns. Once you possess the Kingdom, you possess all the additions. No wonder, the Psalmist declared:

"I have been young, now I'm old, I have never seen the righteous forsaken nor his children begging bread." There is nobody who sought the Kingdom of God, got it and remain a poor man. The kingdom of God comes with additional blessings. Immediately you invest your resources in seeking and obtaining God's kingdom, every other blessings shall be added unto you. Seekers of the heavenly Kingdom will always end up reaping several other benefits. When you seek spiritual blessings, God will give them to you with material blessings added to them. It is impossible for you to seek God's kingdom properly and have no benefit added to you.

Key No. 3

Go out of your way to be a blessing unto others: This is one powerful key to prosperity. God blesses those who are channels of blessings to others. Do not wait until someone begs you for help or assistance, identify those who are in need and go out of your way to bless them. The children of the generous are never poor. God shall water those who water others. Givers never lack. Those who bless others sacrificially shall never lack the good things of life. Bible characters who were mightily blessed were men and women who went out of their ways to bless others.

Key No. 4

Pay your tithes faithfully: You must be a faithful tither if you want to experience prosperity. Tithing should not be approached as an obligation which you must do only when it is convenient. Faithfulness must be your watchword. You must take cognizance of the fact that faithfulness in tithing places you on the pedestal of partnership with the God of heaven and earth. You must pay your tithes even when it appears inconvenient.

Key No. 5

Become an incurable giver: Don't hoard what God has graciously given to you. Those who are generous always receive abundance from God. Those who are stingy will always experience insufficiency. When God makes things available to you, don't pile them up: share them with the needy. It does not make any sense for you to have more than 200 shirts at home when those around you go about with faded and torn dresses. Give. The more you give the more blessings you will receive from God.

Key No. 6

Give your offerings faithfully: The Bible teaches that one of our obligations as believers is the giving of offerings. Offerings differ from tithes. You are expected to give your offerings and pay your tithes. Freewill offerings are an avenue for throwing wide open unto you extra doors of prosperity. Your tithe is a debt. It belongs to God. You must also give your offerings regularly. God has commanded that you must come to His house with your tithes and your offerings.

Key No. 7

Sow seeds: This is referred to as seed offering. You can pave the way for your breakthroughs by specifically sowing seeds. You are expected to take a substantial amount of money and go to God by faith and prayer stating that the financial seed you are sewing is for securing a particular breakthrough. You can promote divine blessings through such seed offerings. Locate an area in which you desire divine intervention, sow a seed in the house of God concerning it and you will be surprised to discover that such a needed miracle will be secured with dispatch. This method of experiencing divine prosperity has been tested and proven times without number. Try God today and He will surprise you.

Key No. 8

Take care of the poor: Divine prosperity has been reserved for those who give their finances for the care of the poor. The Bible teaches specifically that those who take care of the poor shall never lack.

Key No. 9

Pray wealth releasing and transferring prayers: There are certain mysteries in the Scripture. The Bible as reveals that the wealth of the gentiles shall be transferred to the saints.

Isaiah 61:6 - But ye shall be named the priests of the LORD: men shall call you the Ministers of our God: ye shall eat the riches of the gentiles, and in their glory shall ye boast yourselves.

Pray wealth-transferring prayer points. Pray specifically for the transfer of the wealth of the gentiles unto you.

Key No. 10

Work hard: Laziness cannot attract prosperity. You must work hard if you want to get to the realm of prosperity and stay there. Whatever career you have chosen and whatever your line of business, you require a great deal of hard work if you want to be prosperous. Even if God had promised to bless you, you need to work hard in order to experience what God has promised you.

Key No. 11

Avoid the debt trap: It is quite easy to pile up debts but uneasy to get off the hook of indebtedness. Don't live above your means. As much as you can avoid obtaining goods and services on credit. Simply pay for what you can afford and avoid the lure of the "buy now, pay later" scheme. Those who live in advanced countries are daily inundated with adverts soliciting for those who are ready to acquire houses, vehicles, electronic gadgets and even holiday facilities through the credit system. Clients are offered these for installment payments. Before the clients know what is happening they are caught in the intricate web of multiple debts. Hence, many of these people spend their lives paying debts.

Key No. 12

Invest wisely: Office workers, contractors and those who are involved with business and consume their entire earnings and profits. People will end up working and never able to leave an inheritance for their offsprings. The secret of prosperity is investment. No matter how much you have, you will face financial challenges. All you need to do is to be principled. You must invest a portion of your earnings on a regular basis. Wise investment will not only bring back what you invested, it will also attract profit. You should invest in businesses that are not questionable as well as in stocks. You need a measure of education to be able to make sensible or wise investments. You need to prayerfully ask God to guide you.

Key No. 13

Pay your first fruit offerings: This is our main subject. It is an area where there is a lot of ignorance in Christendom today. Most believers know little or nothing concerning this subject, although the Scriptures have quite a lot to say on it. Those who have discovered the mystery behind it have continued to enjoy divine prosperity. Right from the opening pages of the Scriptures, God reveals to us the benefits of first fruit offerings.

Exodus 34:26 - The first of the firstfruits of thy land thou shalt bring unto the house of the LORD thy God. Thou shalt not seethe a kid in his mother's milk.

The first lesson, which we should learn concerning the first fruit offering is that it must be brought to the house of the Lord. More light is thrown on this all-important subject in other Scriptures:

Leviticus 23:10-11 - Speak unto the children of Israel, and say unto them, When ye be come into the land which I give unto you, and shall reap the harvest thereof, then ye shall bring a sheaf of the firstfruits of your harvest unto the priest: And he shall wave the sheaf before the LORD, to be accepted for you: on the morrow after the sabbath the priest shall wave it.

It is amazing to discover here that the first fruits cover things like barley and corn. God was so meticulous that He asked farmers to bring the first fruits unto Him. As if that was not enough, the Lord stated:

Lev. 23:16-17 - Even unto the morrow after the seventh sabbath shall ye number fifty days; and ye shall offer a new meat offering unto the LORD. Ye shall bring out of your habitations two wave loaves of two tenth deals: they shall be of fine flour; they shall be baken with leaven; they are the firstfruits unto the LORD.

In the above Scripture the Lord asked for the first fruits of the harvest of wheat. This shows us that no one is exempted from the first fruits offering. Deut. 18:4 further highlights the scope for the first fruit offering.

Deut. 18:4 - For these nations, which thou shalt possess, hearkened unto observers of times, and unto diviners: but as for thee, the LORD thy God hath not suffered thee so to do.

The Lord does not want you to miss out on the blessings of the first fruit offering. Whether you are trading in corn, oil or poultry, you must give your fruit offering to the Lord. The world-class businessman, the petty trader, the university professor and the owner of a multinational company are all expected to give their first fruit offerings.

Lev. 19:23 - And when ye shall come into the land, and shall have planted all manner of trees for food, then ye shall count the fruit thereof as uncircumcised: three years shall it be as uncircumcised unto you: it shall not be eaten of.

God instructed the children of Israel to dedicate fruit from trees as first fruit offerings unto Him. They were to leave everything until the fifth year in order to enjoy divine increase. Note that your increase may not come until you have offered your first fruit offering unto the Lord. Your financial explosion may not take place until you have given God your first fruit offerings. There are lots of revelations in the Scripture which many believers have glossed over. Ignorance of these mysteries or revelations has been responsible for poverty among God's people.

OBEDIENCE IS THE KEY
No matter how many prayer points you have prayed and how many vigils you have observed, you may remain poor if you disobey divine instructions. God specially attach some levels of prosperity to the first fruit offering. Only those who discover the mysteries and carry out the instructions to the letter can attain these levels.

Ignorance will keep you perpetually in the camp of the poor. You cannot experience the expected breakthrough to prosperity without making use of the mystery of the first fruit offering. God wants you to jump out of the doldrums and join the company of those who enjoy stupendous wealth.

This is your season of prosperity; this is the time you have been waiting for. You must take certain steps to provoke God to bless you like never before.

Deut. 26:2 - That thou shalt take of the first of all the fruit of the earth, which thou shalt bring of thy land that the LORD thy God giveth thee, and shalt put it in a basket, and shalt go unto the place which the LORD thy God shall choose to place his name there.

Here, we are given specific instructions and directions concerning the manner of offering our first fruits. If you are a diligent reader of the Bible you would have discovered that there are no rooms for irrelevancies in the Scriptures. Whenever instructions were given, either in the Old or the New Testament, the details are important. Those who want to give their first fruit offerings are commanded to take what they want to offer to the priests.

You are expected to speak certain words:

Deut 26:3 - And thou shalt go unto the priest that shall be in those days, and say unto him, I profess this day unto the LORD thy God, that I am come unto the country which the LORD sware unto our fathers for to give us.

What you speak when you are giving your first fruit offering is very important. You can tell the Lord something like: "Father, I lived in bondage and served the devil before you saved and delivered me. I was jobless and had no source of income until you blessed me and provided for my needs. I have come to offer my first fruits, "O Lord, I give you praise and worship your Majesty as I give this unto you."

You must pray with faith in your heart as you carry out what God reveals concerning the first fruit offering.

We are given further insight to what the first offering is all about in Numbers 18:12:

Numbers 18:12 - All the best of the oil, and all the best of the wine, and of the wheat, the first fruits of them which they shall offer unto the LORD, them have I given thee.

THE GUIDELINES
Besides giving God our first fruits, we must give Him the very best. Do not offer God the first fruit only when your income is low or when what you are offering means nothing to you. Are the best ones your gain? He deserves the very best. For example, if you are selling clothes, you can decide to pick up the best ones, sell them and bring the money to the Lord.

People ask a lot of questions concerning the manner

of giving our first fruit offerings. The Bible gives us various guidelines concerning this. In the book of Ezekiel specific instructions are given to guide us.

Ezekiel 48:14 - And they shall not sell of it, neither exchange, nor alienate the firstfruits of the land: for it is holy unto the LORD.

The first fruit is holy unto the Lord. It is the exclusive preserve of the Almighty; do not make use of what belongs to God. It is consecrated. As you give it to Lord, He will bless you beyond your wildest dreams.

The best thing to do with your first fruit is to honour the Lord with it. This is clearly stated in Proverb 3:9:

Proverb 3:9 - Honour the LORD with thy substance, and with the firstfruits of all thine increase:

The Bible also says:

Deuteronomy 18:4 - The first fruits also of thy corn, of thy wine, and of thine oil, and the first of the fleece of thy sheep, shalt thou give him.

A GENERAL PROVISION
The Lord does not want anybody to miss out on His blessings.

Leviticus 19:23-25 - And when ye shall come into the land, and shall have planted all manner of trees for food, then ye shall count the fruit thereof as uncircumcised; three years shall it be as uncircumcised unto you; it shall not be eaten of. But in the fourth year all the fruit thereof, that it may yield unto you the increase thereof; I am the Lord your God.

Even for new trees, the first fruits must be given, so that you can have an increase.

Deuteronomy 26:2 - That thou shalt take of the first of·all the fruit of the earth, which thou shalt bring of thy land that the Lord thy God giveth thee, and shalt put in a basket, and shalt go unto the place which the Lord thy God shall choose to place his name there.

You should put your first fruit in an enclosure.

Deuteronomy 26:3-11 - And thou shalt go unto the priest that shall be in those days, and say unto him, I profess this day unto the Lord thy God, that I am come unto the country which the Lord sware unto our fathers for to give us. And the priest shall take the basket out of thine hand, and set it down before the altar of the Lord thy God. And thou shalt speak and say before the Lord thy God, A Syrian ready to perish was my father, and he went down into Egypt, and sojourned there with a few, and became there a nation, great, mighty, and populous: And the Egyptians evil entreated us, and afflicted us, and laid upon us hard bondage: And when we cried unto the Lord God of our fathers, the Lord heard our voice, and looked on our affliction, and our labour, and our oppression: And the Lord brought us forth out of Egypt with a mighty hand, and with an outstretched arm, and with great terribleness, and with signs, and with wonders: And he hath brought us into this place, and hath given us this land, even a land that floweth with milk and honey. And now, behold, I have brought the firstfruits of the land, which thou, O Lord, hast given me. And thou shalt set it before the Lord thy God, and worship before the Lord thy God: And thou shalt rejoice in every good thing which the Lord thy God hath given unto thee, and unto thine house, thou, and the Levite, and the stranger that is among you.

THE BEST STOCK

What you have read shows the procedure of the first fruit offering. You cannot put it down without saying anything. You must follow the procedure.

Numbers 18:12 - And the Levites shall lay their hands upon the heads of the bullocks: and thou shalt offer the one for a sin offering, and the other for a burnt offering, unto the LORD, to make an atonement for the Levites.

First fruits must be the best of what you have. For example, if your business is to sell clothes and you say, I don't know how to give the first fruit offering, take the best, sell it and bring the money to the Church.

Ezekiel 48:14 - And they shall not sell of it, neither exchange, nor alienate the firstfruits of the land: for it is holy unto the LORD.

The first fruit offering is not compulsory. It is only for those who want explosion, expansion, supernatural increase, for the Lord to enlarge their coasts. But anybody who wants to die poor should not bother; It is for those who want to attain unusual heights in life.

The Bible says:

Romans 11:16 - For if the firstfruit be holy, the lump is holy.

When you bring out the first, the rest is consecrated to the Lord. The Bible says, "If the first fruit is holy the lump is holy."

I know that there are people who want supernatural explosion in their businesses. Such people must be ready to give their first fruit offering.

THE IMPLICATIONS
Below are the implications of the first fruit offering:
1. Giving our first fruit to God means we are giving him our most cherished possession. God appreciates it when we give Him the best. It is hard, but it shows that you love God.

2. The first fruits represent our commitment to God. Those who are very wise give the best to the Lord but those who disobey the biblical injunction are far away from God.

3. First fruit shows that God is our priority.

4. Under the law, all first things belong to God. It is an ancient secret of prosperity that we have missed in this generation and this has been affecting us negatively. If you read your Bible very well, you will see that believers themselves are called first fruit offerings. The spirit Himself is called first fruit. Christ himself is called first fruit of them that liveth. All those who are referred to as, or called first fruits are prosperity of the Almighty.

5. The first fruit is a lesson on divine exchange asking you to release your Ishmael, so that your Isaac can come.

6. The first fruit is a lesson on dependence. When you say: "Father, I am doing this to depend on you." And this is a new way of understanding stewardship.

7. The first fruit offering ensures a future harvest. But if you don't give it now, there will be no future harvest. This is a revelation that needs to be clear

to your spirit.

8. **It represents a part of the whole.** That is, once you give the first fruit salary for the year, it is like you have given your salary for the next 11 months to God and it is sanctified. The enemy will not be able to touch it. Because the Bible says that when the first part is offered to the Lord, the remaining part is holy unto the Lord. The part you have given will sanctify the entire one that is left.

9. **First fruit in the original Hebrew language is called Bikkurim. It means the promise to come.** Once that first fruit is given, you ignite the promises of God into action. God will begin to work wonders in your finances. Just as God wants the first-borns in the Bible to be dedicated to Him, so He wants first fruits dedicated to Him. A lot of the first borns are not supposed to be dedicated to other things apart from God. But once the firstborn is not dedicated to God, he will be something else. He will have trouble.

As God wants the firstborn, He wants the first fruit of every income. Have you just started working? The first salary belongs to God. Bring it to the house of the Lord and see how rapid your promotion will be. Your promotion will be swift. You will receive special favour.

A SUDDEN LIFT

A brother listened to this kind of message sometime ago. He had no job for a long time, then he managed to get a job. He was borrowing money to pay transport fare to work. The practice in his place of work was to pay the first three months salaries in bulk at the end of the first month and he heard this kind of message. As soon as he received his salaries in bulk, he gave the whole of them as first fruit offering. The devil was telling him: "You will starve. How will you get to work? Take one month pay out of it."

The brother decided to obey God, to give everything to the Lord. Immediately, the service ended, his phone rang. It was his boss. He said: "Hello! How are you? Well, by the time you left the office today, the managing director tendered his resignation. Would you like to take over that position?" He did not know what to say. He was completely shocked. Just outside the gate, he said: "Yes sir." The boss said, "Ok! See you tomorrow." By the time he got to the place of work the next day he got a house, a car, a driver and special allowance. The breakthrough came immediately after he gave his first fruit offering.

Some of us are busy blocking our blessings. You can pray serious, witchcraft-destroying prayers, but if you are very stingy, even if you have been able to deal with the witchcraft powers the demon attacking your finances would remain in place, because you have not taken steps to dismantle it.

WHY YOU MUST GIVE
The practice of first fruit offering and first born dedications can be traced to the foundation of many cultures in the world.

What is called new yam festival in Nigeria is a corruption of the biblical principle of the first fruit offering. What the Lord is saying is this: Every first animal, every first egg laid by your layers and every first issue brought forth by your animal belong to the Lord. If you do not give God your first fruit, the others following behind will not be as profitable as they should be. So, the first fruit will release promotion, leadership and honour into your life. This is a secret which the devil has been hiding from the church.

Genesis 4:3 - And in process of time it came to pass, that Cain brought of the fruit of the ground an offering unto the LORD.

Beloved, it is difficult for me to keep records of people who just read the Prayer Rain, and got God's blessings, and sent the General Overseer a cheque. I remember how I got a cheque for ₦5 million posted to me. The man wrote: "I I have never attended Mountain of Fire and Miracles Ministries and I have never met you before. But I bought a copy of the Prayer Rain and promised God that if I pray from this book and I get a breakthrough, I will send my tithe to the writer of the book."

This is how God works. We put the money into God's work. These are strategies that many Christians who are not as holy and prayerful as us have discovered. It is a spiritual law. The law does not want to know whether you are reading your Bible or sanctified, or you are a serious believer. Once you follow the law, you get the benefits. But if you are very prayerful and live a holy life and you also give your fist fruit offering, then you will enjoy the benefits more.

FINANCIAL EXPLOSION
Your tithes will protect your income from spiritual robbers and will keep the windows of heaven open for you. But your first fruit will determine your promotion. It will determine your increase, growth, expansion and the rate of your enlargement.

Exodus 22:29-30 - Thou shalt not delay to offer the first of thy ripe fruits, and of thy liquors: the firstborn of thy sons shalt thou give unto me. Likewise shalt thou do with thine oxen, and with thy sheep: seven days it shall be with his dam; on the eighth day thou shalt give it me.

The statement here is very clear: God wants the first-fruit.

The first fruit offering is as valid as the tithe. I want you to understand this: when you give the first fruit it sanctifies every other breakthrough that is forthcoming.

ALL ROUND BLESSINGS
By the grace of God I was given a scholarship to study at the University of Lagos. Life at that time was not as difficult as it is now. Feeding was very cheap. When they gave me my scholarship money, I had already imbibed the principle of first fruit offering. I quickly rushed to the house of the Lord and gave everything.

I began to see the goodness of the Lord. Something happened when I sat for the first major examination in that university. One of the most difficult examination in those days was organic chemistry. The subject was so wide that my notes filled two big notebooks. One week to the examination day, one of my notebooks was stolen and nobody was ready to help me. I felt very bad. I started praying and the Lord said I should read the only notebook left. After going through it I went to sleep.

When I got to the examination hall the next morning and looked through all the questions, there was not a single question from the notebook that was stolen. I started feeling sorry for the person who stole my second notebook, because I knew he would spend time reading it. I did not know that when one of the notebooks was stolen, God just wanted me not to sweat unnecessarily reading two big notes. By the time I finished that course, I came out in first class.

Beloved, if you are ready for the blessing of the first fruit, when you get your first salary, whatever they give to you, everything is the first fruit. But if you have not planned for that, deduct just your transport money from it and then give the Lord the rest, no matter how large it is.

If you are a trader, sit down at the end of the first month, calculate your profit and bring it to the Lord. The profit will enlarge all other profits throughout the year. If you have several wares and you cannot calculate your profit, then the first major thing that you sell, bring it to the Lord, and then you will begin to prosper.

BIBLICAL PRINCIPLES
If you are running something like poultry, the first profit you make, or when you sell all the first batch, you can bring it to the Lord. If you are having regular income, the first income for the year belongs to the Lord. If people give you gifts, the first gift you get in the year belongs to the Lord. Give it to the Lord as a

first fruit offering, and watch what He will begin to do throughout the year.

These are secrets of the church which our Pentecostal fathers understood. They utilized them to maximum advantage. But we have neglected them and the enemy has moved in and done all kinds of evil with our finances. We keep complaining when we are actually guilty of neglecting biblical principles.

When you earn a little salary and you sow that little salary, you are planning for maximum expansion and paving way for maximum breakthroughs and financial explosion. What you start with little will begin to increase until your barns will burst forth. Until the barns of God's people overflow they cannot truly be a blessing to others.

THE BENEFITS
If you are giving your first fruit offering what are the benefits which you will derive from the Lord? The benefits to be derived are as follows:

1. Good health.

2. Dominion prosperity: This kind of prosperity comes to you when you give your first fruit offering.

3. **Uncommon favour:** Doors will just open. When you move into any place, even those who do not like you will give unto you.

4. **Uncommon promotion:** Uncommon promotion will come your way.

5. **Double promotion:** This will be your lot. You will be surprised.

6. **Uncommon blessings:** God will bless you in a unique way.

7. **Strangers will bow down before you and be generous unto you when you:** God will command others to bless you.

8. **You will be a source of blessing to your children and your children's children:** Your family will enjoy you.

There are people who have closed their accounts just to sponsor the things of God, but immediately that is done, God arises and begins to bombard them with all kinds of blessings.

Give your first fruit offering today and your blessings will be explode.

The Mystery Of Seed Offering

S eed offering fulfils a differnt purpose and has its own agenda which we must understand.

1 Corinthians 3:6 - I have planted, Apollos watered; but God gave the increase.

God gives increase but men have to plant something to warrant the increase. It is on what is planted that God would give an increase.

Many people come to the house of God. I categorize them into nine.

PILLARS GROUP
In the first group are those we can call pillars. A pillar is a person who worships regularly and freely gives both his time and money. Pillars never leave a building. They stay even when other things are removed. The truth is that you can be a pillar in the house of God if you want.

The second group is called supporters. Those here give their time, money and resources only if they like the general overseer or the pastor.

The third set is made up of people who are called learners. They use the church for activities such as funerals, baptism, naming ceremonies, marriages, but they don't give their time, money or talents to support the church. In this category we find the prayer collectors who just want to pray and get some blessings. But they do not want to contribute or be part of anything.

All they are concerned with is to receive their breakthroughs and then run away. They do not even bother to know how church bills are paid or how the church is run. When they give offerings to God they do so as if they were giving to a beggar in the street. Some of them would fold the money beyond recognition. Others would look for the worst note they have and give to God. Yet they want God to give them uncommon breakthroughs.

In the next category are those we call **special people**. They give help occasionally when they feel like.

At this point I would like you to close your eyes and take this prayer point:

My father, make me a pillar in your house in the name of Jesus.

The **annual people** are in the next category. In those days we usually called them ECN Christians. They come only on Easter day, Christmas day and New year day. They dress very well and look very serious, but they are only in the church annually. Some husbands accompany their families and after that you don't see them again.

The next category is called the **sponge**. Its members take all the blessings that the church can give but give little or nothing to support the church.

The **vagabond people** are in the next category. They are just going from church to church and have no commitment to any church in particular.

The next set is called the **gossips**. They talk freely about everything, both what they know and what they do not know, whether it concerns them or not. They gossip everyday. There are many of such people in the house of God and this is indeed saddening.

The **referees** fall into the last category of my classification. They take offence at everything and are always criticising everything and everybody. They compare and contrast but would not do anything practical to move the place forward.

The truth I want to tell you is that those upon whom God is ready to shower abundance on belong to the first group of people, the pillars.

WHY BELIEVERS ARE POOR

Christians are supposed to be the richest people on earth. But one of the ways the devil is putting many of us into poverty is by making us stingy towards God. A lot of unbelievers who are not as serious and prayerful as many of us are richer simply because they give. They know that once you sow, God waters. One avenue through which the devil has succeeded in keeping believers in poverty is making them fail in the area of giving.

The first thing the Bible talks about is that God would open the windows of heaven and you would have no room to contain it. If you do not pay your tithes the windows of heaven would be closed and abundance would be far from your reach.

When you eat your tithes you are eating your seed. A farmer who consumes his seed will harvest nothing. You must give heaven the material to work upon. You might be complaining of a poor salary but that is when you should even give more. Any money that comes into your hands, whether gifts, or salary etc, a tithes on it belongs to the Almighty God. If you take the the one tenth which God is asking for and put it in your pocket then God will take whatever He wants from you.

When you take God's one tenth from Him then, He will rise up and take the nine tenths from you. This is the main reason   many modern day Christians are poor. There are many Christians who claim to be holy but they don't pay their tithes. Your life can easily be measured in God's thermometer by the way you give to God.

THE VALUE OF YOUR OFFERING

Many years ago, a woman had a dream in which she found herself at the front of a church where people were dropping their offerings. In that revelation the place had the power of changing a person's gift into its real value. The first gentleman who come in dropped a gold coin into the offering plate and immediately the coin touched the plate it became brass. The woman wondered what the meaning could be. Then God told her that the man gave the money so that people could speak good about him.

A lady also came and put in a penny and immediately, it became half of what she put.   The woman asked to know why. God told her that the lady gave just because it was the tradition to give. Later, a little girl came and dropped something equivalent to the Nigerian one naira. Immediately, it became one kobo. The woman asked God why the offering of the very little girl also dropped its value. God told her that she gave the money because her mother ordered her to give. Finally, a poor woman came and dropped a penny and instantly it changed to gold. The woman

asked God why the woman's old and rough coin changed to gold immediately it hit the plate. God told her that the woman gave her all.

This is a serious matter. Your giving is measured by God, based on what is left after you have given and not what you give. There are many Christians who have not given anybody anything all their lives. There are also many Christians who would never venture into putting their hands into someone's pockets in the bus to steal. They are above that, but they are great thieves because they are stealing from God. They don't steal from men but steal from God, which is a greater offence. You need to pay your tithes on everything you get. Whatever is made available to you must be tithed on.

THE BAG WITH HOLES
I made up my mind, many years ago, never to make poverty my lot. Giving closes the door of poverty. You must not fail in your tithing. Unfortunately, the Bible commands that if you are failing in your tithes when you will eventually pay it, you have to add one fifth of it. If you fail to do so, you are just breaking the rule of God. Poverty and devourers would move into such lives. However, whether you like it or not you do pay tithes. Some pay theirs to Pharaoh.

I learnt my lesson a hard way many years back. It

was not that I was not giving my tithes, but that I just forgot it in the envelope where I kept it. I thought I had paid it but it was still in the envelope there. When I was to pay, eventually it started like this: I went to the fuel station and told them to fill the tank of the old bus I was driving then. They filled the tank and collected their money and I drove off.

All of a sudden, after a few minutes, the bus stooped. We pushed but the bus refused to start. While we were wondering and checking for the source of the problem, nobody went to the tank because we had just bought petrol. However, we discovered later that the filling station had sold to me fake fuel. To make matters worse it had knocked the engine. I tried to trace source of the problem. Then I remembered that I had not paid my tithe. I had to pay immediately.

A lot of people are paying their tithes the hard way because they refuse to pay it appropriately. Many people come to church to pray for breakthroughs but feel that ten per cent of their income is too much to pay as tithe. They refuse to give to their Maker. This is a very grievous offence. The enemy may tell you to borrow your tithes. If you do so you have borrowed trouble.

When children of God who are expected to be multi-millionaires are rolling in poverty despite the promise of God, which says that the earth is the Lord's and the fullness thereof, then something is wrong somewhere.

Another area in which many of us have failed is in that of first fruit offering. We make it as a point of duty in the Mountain of Fire and Miracles Ministries to pray over first fruit offerings regularly.

THE MYSTERY OF GIVING
The Bible makes it clear that we should offer our first fruit offerings. We should be very careful as God's children.

Proverb 3:9 - Honour the LORD with thy substance, and with the firstfruits of all thine increase:

In the above passage the Bible tells us that we should honour the Lord with what we have and the first fruits of our increase.

Our regular offering is another area where many of us have failed. The Bible has given us rules guiding regular offerings.

2 Corinthians. 8-9 - For ye know the grace of our Lord Jesus Christ, that, though he was rich, yet for your sakes he became poor, that ye through his poverty might be rich.

The first rule is that offering is different from the tithe. Tithe is not negotiable at all. And the Bible says if we want to give offerings we should give selflessly. The second rule, according to the Bible, is that we should give consistently. The third, the Bible says, is that we should give willingly. Don't wait until you are pressurised before you give. Don't wait for someone to pick up the microphone and say "I need ₦10million" before you give. Give willingly.

Fifth, give lovingly. Sixth, give proportionately, that is according to your income. Seventh, give cheerfully. The Bible says that God loves a cheerful giver. Eighth, give systematically. Have a programme that would enable you give as regularly as possible. Ninth, give at every opportunity you have. Whenever you are giving to God, do it with excitement. Offering is the key to super-abundance. That is what Christians do not know. When God had a need on earth He sent Jesus to come. When He came the need was met. We must learn from this.

What is a seed?

A seed is a source, a beginning, a propagative structure, a fountain, a conception, a nucleus, an egg. When you sow your seed it has the capacity for enabling you to receive your breakthrough. The Bible tells us: "Whatsoever a man sows, that shall he also reap." Your seed is genetically coded to give you what you want. Every seed has the right substance in it. As small as it is, there is a whole forest in it. It is a powerful thing for someone desiring mighty and uncommon breakthroughs. In fact, the word breakthrough is derived from the sowing concept. When a seed breaks up through the ground it is an evidence of a breakthrough.

When does a believer really sow a seed? You can sow a seed when you want to start any major project in your life. Your seed has life in it that would enable it yield fruits. That seed is God's recovery strategy. It will bruise the head of your serpent.

A CHALLENGE
Are you planning to start a big business or aiming at a divine financial explosion? Give something substantial to God. Sow it as a seed and tell God: "As I start this project there would be an explosion." Try God and He will surprise you.

I remember the story of a woman vividly. Exactly two weeks to her wedding the husband to be declared: "I am sorry, my mother came to me this morning and said a prophet told her that you are a witch, and that if I marry you death is the answer. Therefore, we can no longer be married." The sister was confused. However, she told the man that she was not a witch but a child of God. The man insisted that he would abide by what his mother said that the prophet told her. He asked her to return his engagement ring and ordered her never to see him again. The sister left the place dejected, but she understood the principle of sowing a seed.

The sister had three bank accounts. She went and withdrew everything she had in the three accounts and offered the money to God saying, "I am facing a challenge. God, I am sowing this seed so that it would go and scatter all the challenges I am facing." She did this on a Wednesday and by the time she returned from the church on Sunday, there was a group of people from the man's family waiting to apologise to her. This is one of the benefits that can accrue to you if you sow a seed when you are facing a challenge.

You can also sow a seed when you are facing defeat or loss. David sowed a seed in 1 Samuel 20.

He sowed a seed over the life of a young man whom he saw dying at the war front and it was that young man who took him to where he conquered his enemies. The seed he sowed brought him victory.

SACRIFICIAL GIVING
I remember when I was studying in England on scholarship and they were giving Nigerian students on scholarship 300 pounds per month. I was very happy and contented because the money was more than enough for me. I kept doing praise worship and thanking God for it. But one day as I left the laboratory where I was doing my research I met an Arab student from

Kuwait who was crying bitterly at the corridor. He was lamenting that those who gave them scholarship wanted them to starve. "They are not looking after us. Neither are they taking care of us. How can they expect me to survive on this small money?" he soliloquized.

I was baffled and I asked him: "Sir, do did you say they are giving you small money?" He said, "Yes, how do they expect us to survive on this?". Then I asked, "Sir, how much are they giving you?" To my shocking surprise he said, "Only 10,000 pounds. I had to beckon on him to repeat himself and he repeated: "Only 10,000 pounds." At that point I was shocked to my marrows. While I was rejoicing over 300 pounds another person was lamenting over 10,000 pounds. Then I began to think whether I would be able to meet up with the 300 pounds.

Incidentally, the Lord told me that when I received the 300 pounds, I should remove only my house rent and my feeding allowance and sow the remaining money into the lives of poor students. I obeyed. When I returned from England, my colleagues, even those who were not as brilliant as I was, bought different types of flashy cars, but I came back with nothing. I told them that I sowed my money into the needs of other people and they laughed. However, to the glory of God, the seed which I sowed then is still yielding good fruits now.

You need to sow a seed when you are emphatically serious on getting explosive breakthroughs. All you need to do is to speak to the seed and drop it for God. If you put these principles into practice it would transform your life. The Bible says that whatever a man soweth that shall he also reap. But because we are Christians we would reap bountifully. When you sow a seed you unlock a thousand harvests that you would have concluded would be impossible. This is a very serious issue which I want you to understand.

A GLORIOUS HARVEST

As the General Overseer of the Mountain of Fire and Miracles ministries, I have authored a lot of books and sometimes when these books are sold all the money realised go back into the work of God. And as I put the money into the work of God a multiplication effect follows.

Sometime ago someone whom I did not know sent me a cheque for ₦5million with a testimony. The testimony read: "Dear Dr. Olukoya, I do not know you. Neither have I met you before. But I bought a copy of the Prayer Rain when things were terribly bad for me. Then I prayed to God and told him that if I use this book to pray and receive my breakthrough I would give the writer of the book a certain amount of money. Now that I got my breakthrough, this is my row."

Up till today, I do not know the fellow. This is exactly what happens when you sow a seed. Seed offering is planting a seed in faith with the expectation a specific result. It is anything you receive from God but decide to give back to Him. You can sow your time or money. Seed offering is the tool that God has given to you to create uncommon breakthroughs for yourself. Even if things were not going on well you can give a sacrificial seed offering. Then you can wait for the result.

A SACRIFICIAL OFFERING

There was a woman who happened to be in a church where they were contributing towards the development of the church. Unfortunately for the woman she did not have anything to give. But one day, she came to the church and dropped what was like the biggest offering and the pastor was surprised. The pastor called her and asked her how come she came to the church and dropped what was like the biggest offerings, where she got such an amount of money. She replied that when she discovered that she could not give anything to God when others were giving, she went and sold herself as a slave and that it was the money she contributed.

The woman sold herself for a sacrificial offering unto God. Within a few years she became super rich.

Your seed offering is something that was given to you by God to sow into his work in order for you to secure your future. It is when you let go of whatever is in your hands that God will let go of what is in His own hands.

When the small boy in the Bible released the few loaves and fishes in his hand multiplication took place. Your seed offering is an invisible catalyst for your breakthroughs.

In the Bible, Elijah told the woman to bring the bread and the oil in her hand. The woman replied that it was all that was left for her and her son to eat and die. But she nevertheless gave them to prophet Elijah. What that woman did was sowing a seed into the prophet of God and immediately she sowed that seed the effect of multiplication came along with it. The prophet of God had blessed her and declared that the oil would not finish.

Every seed has an instruction to carry out an assignment for you. There are lots of people who have never in their lives given any seed offering and they wonder why things are not working well for them. Many people who run businesses do not even pay their tithes, therefore their businesses do not grow.

SOWING AND REAPING

When you increase the size of your seed you are

also increasing the size of your harvest. Your seed is your escape route to an uncommon harvest. Also when a man or a woman sows in a time of uncommon hardship, then such a person is getting prepaid abundance. It is not part of the programmes of God for you to be poor, neither is it for you to remain a mediocre. God has an agenda for His people and we must pursue that agenda.

One question I have been asking myself is this: why do Christians pray standing on bare, uncemented floor when they have enough money to cement the floor of the church? Many believers are stingy. The principle of the Bible concerning giving is not to let your left hand know what your right hand is doing. If you are waiting for someone to publicise that they need your assistance in the church, then you are barring yourself from multiple blessings. But those who give to God without invitation or pressure are preparing for uncommon breakthroughs.

Beloved, begin to give as from today. Sow special seed offerings and make it sacrificial. Speak to the seed, order it to make it work for your and bring forth abundance into your life. Sow it into the things of God and see what happens.

Sometime ago, a white missionary friend of mine told us a story of what happened when he went to minister in India. He saw a woman who was going to worship her idol in the river and tried to persuade her not to worship the river but all to no avail. The woman had a very sick child and another healthy one. She headed to the river with the two children. He wanted to donate one of them to the idol. The white missionary thought that since she had two children and one of them was sick, she would throw the sick one to her idol and then come back. However, when the woman was coming back the white man was shocked to discover that she was returning with the sick child. When he asked her why she sacrificed the healthy child, "I will not give my idol a sick sacrifice," she replied. This was an idol worshipper who would not give her idols a sick sacrifice. How much more should those of us who are worshipping the true God give our God healthy sacifices.

The Mystery Of Giving

Several years ago, the Lord gave me a strong prophetic word concerning members of the Mountain of Fire and Miracles Ministries. He said they would be the richest Christians in the world. No doubt God has blessed many of our members. These members have been able to key into what was said at that time and they are all rejoicing now. In recent times, God again spoke concerning His plans to enrich members of the Mountain of Fire and Miracles Ministries with stupendous wealth.

I took quite a few complaints to the Lord about our members and He said His promise that they would be the richest around was still valid. He said there were deep truths I must teach, part of the reason that some people are wobbling in abject poverty or fail at the edge of great financial breakthroughs. That is what I am teaching in this chapter.

The Bible says:

Luke 6:38 - Give, and it shall be given unto you; good measure, pressed down, and shaken together, and running over, shall men give into your bosom. For with the same measure that ye mete withal it shall be measured to you again.

A COMMAND

The Bible commands you to give. It is not an advice. It is a command. Give and it shall be given unto you. Every good thing starts with giving. All other things are attachments. "Give and it shall be given....." the Bible declares.

The measure with which you give is what shall come to you. The reverse is also true. Refrain from giving and keep what you have and you remain in poverty. Let me examine other passages on the importance of giving.

Acts 20:35 - I have shewed you all things, how that so labouring ye ought to support the weak, and to remember the words of the Lord Jesus, how he said, It is more blessed to give than to receive.

2 Corinthians 9:6-7 - But this I say, He which soweth sparingly shall reap also sparingly; and he which soweth bountifully shall reap also bountifully. Every man according as he purposeth in his heart, so let him give; not grudgingly, or of necessity: for God loveth a cheerful giver.

Proverb 11:24-25 - There is that scattereth, and yet increaseth; and there is that withholdeth more than is meet, but it tendeth to poverty. The liberal soul shall be made fat: and he that watereth shall be watered also himself.

All these scriptures are saying only one thing: Give and get; keep and lose.

IMPORTANT FACTS
Let me now give you some facts about giving.

1. **The hand that gives will gather. The hand that gives gathers. So, if there is famine around you, check the level of your offering.**

2. **Trying to cheat God is bad economy. When God says bring and you don't bring, but you are trying to cheat the Almighty, it is a very bad economy. And when God wants to measure what you are giving unto Him, He measures it by what you have left behind after you have given to Him. He does not measure by what you have offered.**

We have lots of lessons to learn from these events. The truth is that if you cannot give to the Lord when you are poor, you won't give when you are rich. So trying to cheat God is trying to build on the platform of poverty.

3. **Two qualities make a Christian to stand out. They are giving and forgiving.**

4. **What you give lives on.**

5. **Giving is the thermometer of our love for God.**

Why do you claim to love Jesus and when it comes to giving to Him you treat Him as a beggar. Why act as if you were giving somebody who gave you a good service at the restaurant a tip. Many believers are poor because they do not follow these principles despite their being holy. Some Christians whose prayer life and holy lifestyle are below those of others are richer because they understand the divine principles of giving and are giving. When you give, God begins to open doors for you.

6. **Giving is God's medicine for greed.** If you are giving, that is a cure for greed.

7. **An offering is faith in action.** Any offering you give makes you to put your faith into action. The tithe is God's own. You are not giving Him, you are paying a debt you owe. If you want the windows of heaven to be open, you must activate it.

8. **Giving impresses God because God Himself is a giver.** The Bible says: "God so loved the world that He gave..."

9. **Your uncommon sowing will create an uncommon harvest for you.** When you are really ready for uncommon financial breakthroughs, you will do uncommon sowing. Your uncommon sowing will produce an uncommon harvest for you.

10. **Giving is a divine attribute and those who give are God-like.** When you give you are manifesting God's attribute.

11. **God promises to respond to giving.** "Give and it shall be given unto you." Give …….get; keep……lose.

12. **Giving is love in action.**

They took contributions in one church because they wanted to build. A poor little girl there cried as she considered what to give. Then she remembered that they willed a golden ring to her. That was the only thing that her rich grandparents willed to her. She kept it to her heart. That gold ring was a lot of money. Since she didn't have money to give, she put in the golden ring into the offering box. By the time they collected the offering they found that they had more than enough and did not need the ring. The pastor called her saying: "Sorry, we have enough money, so you don't have to contribute this expensive ring. You can have it back. She snapped at the pastor in anger: "Pastor, I did not give that ring to you, I gave it to God."

Many present day believers would have collected the ring, and that would have blocked their blessings. That little girl became one of the greatest women of God.

13. **God treasures the giver.** Once you are a giver, God sees you as a treasure and there are many tragedies that would just fly over you.

One day, when we were not yet large in number in MFM, one brother shared an unfortunate testimony. He had learnt his lessons the hard way. Any time they were giving offering, he never gave anything. However, as he prayed over and over again, God gave him a job, better than what he was doing before. But they did not pay them until about three months. Meanwhile, he had used up his savings.

Then when he collected his fat salary he was rejoicing and planning what to do with it. He thought he was very clever as he hid the money inside his stockings and wore his shoes so that there would be no way he could lose the money. He took a commuter bus that day. Hoodlums waylaid him. They said: "You have to give us something. He replied, " I don't have anything. There is nothing here." They said, "So, you don't have anything? Would you agree that if we search your pockets and find anything there we should take it?" He told them to go ahead.

They searched the first and second pockets but found nothing. They were about to tell him to go when one of them noticed his swollen stockings. They asked him if he was suffering from elephantiasis. At that level, he started shaking. They took off his stockings, the money poured out and they took everything. He cried at the bus-stop until his voice became hoarse. Later he came to give this testimony and advised that those who would want to copy him should never do so.

Why did God not protect him? Because he was not a giver.

14. The treasures you keep in heaven are laid up. The treasures you keep on earth are laid down.

15. If you are a lazy giver, you will be a lazy receiver. The same lazy way in which you give is the lazy way it would be returned to you.

16. There are three kinds of giving:
. People who hate to give, give grudgingly.
· Duty giving.
· Thanksgiving.

17. If you want to change what you are getting from heaven, then change what you are giving.

18. You have to sow before you can reap. That is what the Bible teaches.

19. There is nobody in the Bible who gave and did not receive more than he gave.

20. Nothing will be yours until you are ready to give. If you have never given, nothing will be yours. When you begin to give, God will embarrass you with prosperity.

21. Whatever you keep to yourself, you will eventually lose. But what you give to the Lord, you will keep forever.

22. If you sow much; you will reap much. If you sow little you will reap little.

23. The more you give to God, the more you will get. As you give out, you will receive.

24. Giving gives true wealth. That is when you have genuine wealth.

25. We become rich only through what we give, and remain poor through what we keep and refuse to give. Give and become rich today.

26. The Dead Sea is dead because it continually receives and never gives. In the Dead Sea, no animal is alive because it receives but never gives.

It is the same thing when you receive and you never give. You will be dead.

27. **Giving opens uncommon doors.** All those who are mightily blessed in the Bible were men and women who went out of their ways to be blessings unto others. If the widow of Zarephat were a stingy woman when Elijah came and asked for cups of water and a morsel of bread in her hand, she would have refused. Her refusal would have led to closed doors. But her giving opened uncommon doors for her. Peter also went out of his way and gave his boat and uncommon doors opened unto him.

28. **Prayer is mentioned 500 times in the New Testament.** Faith is mentioned less than 500 times. Giving is mentioned over 2000 times. Out of the 38 parables of Jesus, 16 dealt with giving. Giving is therefore a serious divine principle.

29. **Giving is an act of obedience when you want to obey the Lord.** You don't consider your convenience. If you are supposed to give and you do not give, the blessing that is supposed to come to your life so that you can be a blessing unto others will not arrive. Then you will be held responsible in heaven for your disobedience.

I read a story that touched my life. They were raising a missionary fund in one church. There was one poor woman who couldn't give anything and it pained her. But after one week she came with a large sum of money, the kind of money that would take even people who are working almost one year to raise, the pastor was surprised and asked to know where she got the money. Later the pastor found out what she did. This woman sold herself as a slave and got the money she offered in the church. A free person became a slave because she wanted to obey God; because she wanted to contribute meaningfully to the work of God.

Giving sacrificially is a principle that can never be put aside by those who want mighty blessings.

30. Giving is an act of worship.

2 Sam. 24:24-25 - And the king said unto Araunah, Nay, but I will surely buy it of thee at a price: neither will I offer burnt offerings unto the LORD my God of that which doth cost me nothing. So David bought the threshingfloor and the oxen for fifty shekels of silver. And David built there an altar unto the LORD, and offered burnt offerings and peace offerings. So the LORD was intreated for the land, and the plague was stayed from Israel.

David paid for what the man wanted to give him

free because he didn't want to give God what would cost him nothing. Old Testament people understood the principles of giving which people of these generations do not understand. What will count is what you lay up as treasures in heaven.

31. **Giving is not a contribution.** It is an eternal investment.

32. **In order to have great opportunities you must do an uncommon sowing.** Sow your money in order to have great opportunities.

I come from a very poor home and my parents did not have any money to even buy a ticket to go from Lagos to Port Harcourt by air. But the first money I made in my life, appeared big but I took it to my pastor. He looked at the money and said, "Where did you get this?" I said, "That is my first salary." He told me to kneel down. I didn't know that some people were crying on his neck. The pastor cried out his heart in prayer and I saw the effect. Do an uncommon sowing and see what the Lord will do for you.

33. **Your money is a seed.** A seed is a tiny beginning with a huge future. But the mistake most people make about seed offering is that they give things that do not really hurt them.

34. **You cannot outdo God in giving.** Giving to God is like putting your money in the best bank. God, as an economist, will lavish a larger gifts upon those who give to Him.

35. **One great reason for our poverty is stinginess towards God.** God withholds from us when we withhold from Him.

36. **Giving is God's way of raising wealthy men and women.**

37. **Giving should be done as you would give if Jesus Christ were the usher standing in front of you.**

38. **He who gives quickly gives twice.**

39. **Only 15 percent of the members of an average church carry the financial load of the church.** Are you one of the givers?

40. **We all pay tithes either to God or to Pharaoh.** So, if you don't pay your tithe to God, things like adversity or unemployment will take away. And it is a tragedy.

When we are giving to God, all we are doing is taking our hands off what belongs to Him. When you take what God does not want you to have, He will take what you are supposed to have. The way you use your money shows what you think of the Lord your God.

41. Many believers have been caged by the spirit of mammon. Money has put human beings into the battles that have no end. It has been the subject of pursuit since men came into the world. It has turned itself into the greatest idol. It is a deceiver. It will give sicknesses that nobody can remove. Money is a confusionist because those who do not have it think they are in trouble. Money has deceived so many girls into sacrificing their virginity and wasting their virtues. Money has made many to suck blood in strange places. Money has changed the vision of so many innocent souls to the grave yard. Money has turned so many women to widows. Money has turned so many children to orphans. Money has a caging influence, a dominating evil power, a destructive hand.

42. Your life is more than money. You met money in this world and one day you will leave it behind. Money should not dispatch you out of this world before your time. As a Christian, money is made for you, you are not made for money. Quick money is quick death. As a Christian, you are supposed to be hard-working and sincere and get the blessings of the Lord. There has never been any peace in wrong money. Money has a voice. To listen

to his voice is to marry a cobra. Money is strong and deceitful. It controls fools and make them do all kinds of evil. Money that does not come from God is not a blessing. There is a spiritual force behind money.

As a believer one of your key Scriptures should be Rom 12:1:

Romans 12:1 - I beseech you therefore, brethren, by the mercies of God, that ye present your bodies a living sacrifice, holy, acceptable unto God, which is your reasonable service.

Your concentration on the Lord determines the kind of Christian you are.

Matt 27:3-4 - Then Judas, which had betrayed him, when he saw that he was condemned, repented himself, and brought again the thirty pieces of silver to the chief priests and elders, saying, I have sinned in that I have betrayed the innocent blood. And they said, What is that to us? see thou to that.

Money destroyed Judas Iscariot. Do not allow money to destroy you. Give and be blessed.

The Mystery Of The Book Of Remembrance

There are several books mentioned in the 'Book of books', the Bible. The meaning of these books may not be clear to us. In this chapter we shall be looking at only one of these mystery books. I want you to pay attention to this mystery and use it as a ladder to posses your possessions.

Let us first take a cursory look at some of the books referred to in the Scriptures.
There is one book, which the Bible refers to as the book of wars:

Number 21:14 - Wherefore it is said in the book of the wars of the LORD, What he did in the Red sea, and in the brooks of Arnon,

Not much is known of the book of wars. There is another book mentioned in Daniel 12:1:

Daniel 12:1 - And at that time shall Michael stand up, the great prince which standeth for the children of thy people: and there shall be a time of trouble, such as never was since there was a nation even to that same time: and at that time thy people shall be delivered, every one that shall be found written in the book.

The book referred to in the above passage is the book of life. This is the same book we will find in Revelation 20:12.

Revelation 20:12 - And I saw the dead, small and great, stand before God; and the books were opened: and another book was opened, which is the book of life: and the dead were judged out of those things which were written in the books, according to their works.

In the above passage there is another book called the book of judgement. It can also be found in Daniel 7:10:

Daniel 7:10 - A fiery stream issued and came forth from before him: thousand thousands ministered unto him, and ten thousand times ten thousand stood before him: the judgment was set, and the books were opened.

Human books might tell lies because the lawyers and judges of this world are not perfect. They might make mistakes. But the book we are talking about in this message is a book free from errors and mistakes.

Revelation 5:1 - And I saw in the right hand of him that sat on the throne a book written within and on the backside, sealed with seven seals.

Revelation 10:2 - And he had in his hand a little book open: and he set his right foot upon the sea, and his left foot on the earth.

THE BOOK OF REMEMBERANCE

However, the specific book we will be focusing on is found in Malachi 3:16:

Malachi 3:16 - Then they that feared the LORD spake often one to another: and the LORD hearkened, and heard it, and a book of remembrance was written before him for them that feared the LORD, and that thought upon his name.

The book of remembrance is in the hands of the Almighty. He orders it to be opened and makes things to be written in it. There is something mysterious about this book. God is a God of precision, purpose, timing and plan. He writes things in line with the appointed time.

Anyone who comes into this world comes with a lot of virtues. Certain things were planted into your life before you were born and those things are destined to make you great. But outside this original divine deposit, there are extra things which you can get free of charge. God has records of these extra deposits.

There are some things that people do and God shows them special favour. God then writes those things down on their behalf and lists the name of the people for divine blessings. Below are some of the characteristics of the Book of Remembrance:

a) **God gives attention to what is in it.** This is why in this world it is good to be good because anything you do has a reward, weather it is good or bad. The Bible makes us know that everyone would stand before the judgement seat of Christ to give account of what he has done on earth, weather it is good or bad. Every good thing you do goes down into the book of remembrance on your behalf and may help you at one point or the other. The Bible makes us know that God gives detailed attention to whatever is going on among us.

b) **The book tells us that God pays strict attention to what we say.** Therefore, we have to be very careful with what we say. If what we say does not glorify God then we are not doing ourselves any good.

c) **God sees all you do and hears all you say.**

d) **The book makes us know that God is a writer.** He writes down things in this special book.

e) **In Heaven there is a counterpart of what in school we call the black book.** If you commit a grievous offence in school your name is written in that book and once your name is written there you will never obtain any good reference from the school.

In a particular school, there was a black book. One particular day, the principal came into the hall and made a grievous announcement. Two boys had fought and one stuck a knife into the other. The principal took the knife, dried the blood on it, wrote the name of the student who used it in the black book and then put the knife in the boy's file. Each time the Principal comes to the hall to talk to us he would tell the culprit: "The blood of the fellow whom you stabbed is in your hand." Then he would tell us: "If your name happens to be in the black book when you collect your testimonial, it would be so hot to the extent that you will drop it." There is also a book like that in heaven. It is the book of remembrance, but it also records your good deeds.

f)   Any genuine effort anyone contributes, even once, to further the kingdom of God is recorded. Your pastor may not recognise the fact that you are working but it is recorded. People might even say that you are not doing anything but it is recorded.

g)   This book also tells us that there are certain names of certain people that have been recorded for special breakthroughs, such that people would hear and be amazed. When your name is recorded by God the whole world will recognise you.

h)   It also tells us that there is a record of people who would be spared disasters or tragedies. No matter how terrible the disasters or tragedies, they will escape. They are exempted from calamities.

When a book of remembrance is written on your behalf, you will be spared disasters and tragedies.

i)   This book also contains the names of special candidates for special honours.

j)   The book contains a record of special possessions of the Lord. God calls them jewels of the Lord, which He keeps specially.

Esther 6:1-10 - On that night could not the king sleep, and he commanded to bring the book of records of the chronicles; and they were read before the king. And it was found written, that Mordecai had told of Bigthana and Teresh, two of the king's chamberlains, the keepers of the door, who sought to lay hand on the king Ahasuerus. And the king said, What honour and dignity hath been done to Mordecai for this? Then said the king's servants that ministered unto him, There is nothing done for him. And the king said, Who is in the court? Now Haman was come into the outward court of the king's house, to speak unto the king to hang Mordecai on the gallows that he had prepared for him. And the king's servants said unto him, Behold, Haman standeth in the court. And the king said, Let him come in. So Haman came in. And the king said unto him, What shall be done unto the man whom the king delighteth to honour? Now Haman thought in his heart, To whom would the king delight to do honour more than to myself? And Haman answered the king, For the man whom the king delighteth to honour, Let the royal apparel be brought which the king useth to wear, and the horse that the king rideth upon, and the crown royal which is set upon his head: And let this apparel and horse be delivered to the hand of one of the king's most noble princes, that they may array the man withal whom the king delighteth to honour, and bring him on horseback through the street of the city, and proclaim before him, Thus shall it be done to the man whom the king delighteth to honour. Then the king said to Haman, Make haste, and take the apparel and the horse, as thou hast said, and do even so to Mordecai the Jew, that sitteth at the king's gate: let nothing fail of all that thou hast spoken.

In the above passage we see that Mordecai was in trouble. He was to be killed. But he had done something that was written in the king's book of remembrance. On that particular night the king could not sleep. He inquired of the reward that was given to the man for his great act and the people replied that nothing was given to him. At that point Haman surfaced and the king asked him what could be done to such a person. He told the king that the person should be treated like a king. It was the same Haman who had plotted to kill Mordecai that made the suggestion concerning the kind of honour has to be bestowed on Mordecai.

Please, take these prayer points:

1. Any man ordained to bless me and has not done so, let him lose his sleep until he rises up to bless me, in the name of Jesus.

2. My book of remembrance, open by fire, in the name of Jesus.

   Man may forget you. But God will never forget you. The act of forgetting benefactors is common with human beings. They may not remember you but God will open a book of remembrance for you.

Genesis 40:23 - Yet did not the chief butler remember Joseph, but forgat him.

Genesis 41:1-2 - And it came to pass at the end of two full years, that Pharaoh dreamed: and, behold, he stood by the river. And, behold, there came up out of the river seven well favoured kine and fatfleshed; and they fed in a meadow.

Genesis 41:8-13 - And it came to pass in the morning that his spirit was troubled; and he sent and called for all the magicians of Egypt, and all the wise men thereof: and Pharaoh told them his dream; but there was none that could interpret them unto Pharaoh. Then spake the chief butler unto Pharaoh, saying, I do remember my faults this day: Pharaoh was wroth with his servants, and put me in ward in the captain of the guard's house, both me and the chief baker: And we dreamed a dream in one night, I and he; we dreamed each man according to the interpretation of his dream. And there was there with us a young man, an Hebrew, servant to the captain of the guard; and we told him, and he interpreted to us our dreams; to each man according to his dream he did interpret. And it came to pass, as he interpreted to us, so it was; me he restored unto mine office, and him he hanged.

In the above passages we discover that Joseph was totally forgotten until a book of remembrance was open for him. There is no way you can be completely forgotten by human beings as long as God has not forgotten you. God will cause them to remember you.

WHEN THE BOOK IS OPENED
There was also a man in the Bible who prayed his last prayer point and that prayer point was what brought him glory.

Luke 23:42 - And he said unto Jesus, Lord, remember me when thou comest into thy kingdom.

There are some kinds of prayer points you need to pray for the book of remembrance to be opened for you. The moment the book of remembrance is opened you will begin to discover the marvels of divine breakthroughs.

Genesis 8:1 - And God remembered Noah, and every living thing, and all the cattle that was with him in the ark: and God made a wind to pass over the earth, and the waters asswaged;

Genesis 19:29 - And it came to pass, when God destroyed the cities of the plain, that God remembered Abraham, and sent Lot out of the midst of the overthrow, when he overthrew the cities in the which Lot dwelt.

Genesis 30:22 - And God remembered Rachel, and God hearkened to her, and opened her womb.

Exodus 2:24 - And God heard their groaning, and God remembered his covenant with Abraham, with Isaac, and with Jacob.

Psalm 136:23 - Who remembered us in our low estate: for his mercy endureth for ever.

RESULTS OF REMEMBRANCE
From the above passages the conclusion we can draw is that when God remembers you the following will take place in your life:

a)   You will shine.
b)   Your stubborn enemies will be disgraced.
c)   You are sure to have special promotion.
d)   You will have uncommon breakthroughs.
e)   You will experience financial explosion. You will
      be blessed abundantly.

I remember the story of a brother who was very poor and had no money to contribute in the church. But he was present at every prayer meeting and prayed from his heart seriously. One day, somebody pointed at him and said: "You always come here, you attend every meeting and you pray, but when we say people should contribute you do not contribute anything." On hearing this the brother became very depressed and said he was not going to come to that church again, and he left.

THE STONE REJECTED BY BUILDER

Precisely two days later the government wrote to that church saying that the church was obstructing the main road and that they should leave the place with immediate effect. The whole church now started to pray and all of a sudden there was a prophecy. God told them that He gave them an angel in the person of that brother and that it was his voice that He used to hear. "Go and bring him back." God commanded. Immediately the church went in search of the brother, apologised to him and brought him back. A few hours after he came back the government wrote to the church apologising for the first letter which, it said, was a mistake. This brother continued in his fervent prayers and God soon told him that He had remembered him. "You are going to have financial explosion." He was amazed.

One day, as he was coming home from the church the spirit of God told him to walk to the Bar Beach. He obeyed. As he lifted up his eyes he saw a bottle floating on the sea. It was a strange bottle. The spirit of God told him to pick it. Inside the bottle was a tiny piece of paper written by a rich man who had no child nor a family to bequeath his wealth. In fact, the only property the man had was a dog. In his will he divided his property into two. He gave one half to his dog and the other half was for anybody who would find the bottle which he threw into the sea. He said that whoever would present the document in the bottle to the bank, the bank should release half of his property to him. What the brother found changed the course of his history and that of his generations. The man who was once trekking became a man who could travel all over the world by Concord aircraft. God remembered him.

f)   Your enemies will die in your place. That was exactly what happened to Haman when God remembered Mordecai. Haman died in the place he prepared for Modecai. Beloved, there is indeed a book called the Book of Remembrance.

GAINING AN ENTRY

The question now is: How can you get your name into this book? How can you get the book of remembrance to be opened for you?

Malachi 3:16 - Then they that feared the LORD spake often one to another: and the LORD hearkened, and heard it, and a book of remembrance was written before him for them that feared the LORD, and that thought upon his name.

1) The first condition for anyone to get his name into the book of remembrance is that he must fear the Lord. A lot of Christians have lost the fear of the Lord. Many do not have respect for God anymore.

2) Another condition is that you must attend fellowship meetings regularly. You must not abandon or ignore the fellowship of God's children.

3) You must remain true to God and honour His name.

4) You can also pray yourself to the position of being enlisted in God's book of remembrance. There are certain individuals whom God has decided to bless

by His soveign power. He does not want to know weather such people are qualified for such blessings or not. If you cannot operate under that soveign power of God you can pray yourself into a position of favour. These prayers will catapult you to victory, in Jesus' name.

A GREAT CHANGE

It is unfortunate that some believers are mocked by unbelievers who keep saying that despite their Christianity God has not favoured them. The truth is that when the book of remembrance is opened unto such people their story would change. The mockery and the ridicule will be converted to promotion. For some people the enemy has placed a heavy burden upon them and any time they dream they see themselves slaving for others. The truth is that once the book of remembrance is opened to such people they will break their shackles and return the heavy load to the owner.

Perhaps you have been experiencing strange problems, when the book of remembrance is opened unto you, that would mark the end of such problems.

The Mystery Of The Bag With Holes

Haggai. **1:6** - Ye have sown much, and bring in little; ye eat, but ye have not enough; ye drink, but ye are not filled with drink; ye clothe you, but there is none warm; and he that earneth wages earneth wages to put it into a bag with holes.

There is a spiritual entity known as the bag with holes. This bag is not a physical bag or purse which you can see. It is a spiritual bag. Note that every blessing that is available in the physical is first seen in the spiritual. Therefore, every blessing is represented as an entity in the spirit world. When you see the blessing in the spirit realm and it manifests in the physical, then you will begin to enjoy it.

The spirit world first existed before the physical world. That is why Jesus said to his disciple: "Go into the world and preach the gospel, any house you get to, declare that peace be unto it. If a child of peace is in that house, peace shall abide upon him but if a child of peace is not there then your peace will return to you. Here Jesus identified peace as a spiritual entity. The entity called peace is mobile. It can go in and out. Peace is a personality in the spirit realm. A lot of Christians are suffering from spiritual diabetes. They prefer the cushion to the cross. They will want to lay their heads on the lap of Delilah and wake up on the bossom of Abraham.

SPIRITUAL AILMENTS

Many Christians also suffered from what we call spiritual insanity. When you know a particular thing is bad, and it is not God's will, and you go ahead and do it, you are suffering from spiritual madness. There are lots of christians suffering from spiritual madness who go ahead and do what the Lord forbids. When God says, "Thou shall not" and you go ahead and do it, then you are suffering from spiritual madness.

A lot of christians suffer from spiritual blindness. When they come to church, they hear nothing, they see nothing, they prophesy nothing and they don't get into any spiritual action. They are experts at falling into the pit and coming out. They are experts at giving their lives to God today and backsliding tomorrow. They get born again several times. People in this group are spiritually blind. There are many christians with bags of holes over their necks which means they are losing what they are supposed to retain.

The reason so many people, especially christians, experience backwardness, is that they still have in their lives the bag with holes. Backwardness in this sense means continuous consumption of the bread of sorrow. It means operating below divine schedules. Backwardness means abandoning the head for the tail. It means aiming at nothing in life. It means throwing your net into the wrong sea. Backwardness means washing more clothes then you can hang out. It means you are the eraser on your pencil which will wear out before your pencil finishes. It means learning nothing from your mistakes. Backwardness means failing in life in spite of being talented. It means to have several activities, but no achievement.

THE LEAKING BAG
When you concentrate on so many things but you are busy doing nothing, it is backwardness. When you think without purpose, it is backwardness. When you focus on the rear mirror, when you concentrate on the back always, you are guilty of backwardness. When you are a specialist in struggling for leftovers, you are experiencing backwardness.

Backwardness is when God puts you on the weighing balance and you weigh nothing. Backwardness is to form the habit of boasting, sleeping always and laziness.

The terrible spirit called the bag with holes never fades. It is a thirst that cannot be quenched with satisfaction or contentment. Things are getting in but they are leaking out. When the bag with holes is over a person's neck, the person will be delayed in the area of obedience and repentance. Life without Christ or life outside God's kingdom will invite the spirit of the bag with holes. The spirit of vain labour is attached to the spirit of the bag with holes. The effort of trying to get prosperity without God is a spirit of the bag with holes. All the laying of your treasures on earth and not in heaven is the product of the spirit of the bag with holes.

In essence, the bag with holes is a spiritual leakage. The problem is not that christians do not receive blessings. The problem is not that under the anointing certain impossible situations are not made possible. The Bible says, "With men this is impossible but with God all things are possible." The problem is that christians receive these blessings as miracles, in an environment filed with anointing, but the blessings leak out.

SPIRITUAL LEAKAGE

Spiritual leakage makes prayers useless. If other people are receiving outstanding miracles and you are a candidate of the bag with holes, you will not receive any. When people pray for financial breakthroughs and God bombards them with breakthroughs, if there is leakage they are back to square one. They need to pray against the bag with holes. Many come to the stream of God's blessings with baskets. The enemy has replaced so many people's buckets with baskets which cannot retain any water. In His wisdon, the Almighty will not pour water into the baskets until those spiritual holes making goodness and blessings to leak out are sealed. Such people touch blessings but lose them later.

Many are like the fishermen who throw their nets into the sea and catch a fish and the fish struggles and gets off the hook and succeed in throwing itself back into the sea. The bag of your financial blessings may be leaking. You earn money but you don't know how it goes. You work hard but little or no financial gains come your way. You may do some jobs very well but the jobs may slip from your hand all because there is financial leakage in your life. You may get to a level when new buyers are avoiding your own shop and your old customers begin to look for new shops. Problems may keep mounting upon problems with your meager resources.

You need to deliver yourself from the spirit of the bag with holes. When debts surround you like sea, it is a bag with holes. If you pray seriously but you are unable to keep a regular job, you are suffering from the spirit of the bag with holes. When you experience unexplainable loss of money, it is the spirit of the bag with holes. When you experience very serious problem which make you lose your peace, you are suffering from the bag with holes. When you make reasonable income but you are still financially handicapped, it is the bag with holes. When you are always duped or armed robber keep disturbing you, you are suffering from the spirit of the bag with holes.

THE SYMPTOMS

The bag with holes can be attached to somebody's life and the person will be suffering from spiritual diarrhea. Some christians who spoke in tongues can no longer do so because of the spirit of the bags with holes. Christians who used to feel the anointing of God and those who saw visions of the angel of the Lord revealing things to them can no longer feel or see anything because the spirit of the bags with holes is attached to their spiritual lives.

When you notice that past bad dreams are finding their ways back to your life and when you notice that spiritual problems are coming back to your life, then a bag with holes has been attached to your life. Many are unable to memorise scriptures; as they meditate on some Scriptures they keep going away from their memory. This is because a bag with holes is attached to their lives. Some people have been on the same spiritual level for years because the bag with holes has been attached to their lives.

When you don't have the ability to go fully with the Lord, it is an evidence of the bag presence of a bag with holes. When you experience constant failures in examinations, then a bag with holes has been attached to your life. When you experience constant memory failure, you have a bag with holes. Other symptoms include inability to retain good things for a long time, misfortune and unsettled homes. The spirit of the bag with holes is a very clever spirit. People who have the bag with holes, keep losing things. When you experience spiritual leakage, the demons are operating in your life. When you receive blessings and keep handing them over to your enemy, it is the evidence of bag with holes.

LEAKAGE DREAMS

Some people cry to God for blessings and God shows them in the dream that He is giving them but they are losing everthing to the enemy. When you receive blessings in the church and right there in the church you lose your temper and fight, you will lose your blessings.

If you begin to dream that you are obtaining good things but evil powers are ordering you to hand them over to them, and you notice that this happens physically, then it is an evidence that the bag with holes has been attached to your life. When you find yourself in a dream spending lavishly, you collect your salary and you are spending it carelessly, but you don't do so physically, you are a victim of a bag with holes. If you dream of losing money, the bag with holes has been attached to your life. When you have a dream that your pocket is leaking, or you could not find a substantial amount of money, it is an evidence of the problem of a bag with holes.

When in your dream you find yourself counting coins, or your properties are being auctioned in your presence or you search for something important and cannot find, it is an evidence that you are a victim of the attack of a bag with holes. When you are climbing stairs and the stairs seem not to end, or you find yourself plucking unripe or spoilt fruit, then you are having leakage dreams. When you notice that somebody is taking an organ away from your body or pushing a syringe into your body to get some blood from your body, it is an evidence of leakage dreams. When you see yourself blind in one eye or bargaining for an old clothe in the market instead of buying new clothes, or you see yourself being pursued by giants or masquerades, or you see yourself being buried, then you are having leakage dreams.

When in a dream you find your name on a notice board indicating failure in an examination, then the dream is an indication that you have a bag with holes. You can tackle your past or present dreams with violent prayers.

DEMONIC AVENUES
There are powers distributing bags with holes. They

will not stop you from getting blessed; you will accumulate blessings but you will lose them. The law of the bag with holes is that you will accumulate and lose you blessings.

The keywords of spiritual leakage are disappointment and frustration. Beloved, you cannot be a blessing when you are not blessed. So, anything that is making you not to retain your blessings in life, anything that is making the power of God to fail in your life, is the bag with holes.

Brethren, the truth is that the only person who can stop God's promises in your life is you. If you make up your mind that you will command spiritual leakage to die, if you make up your mind to follow divine principles for accumulation, the power of spiritual leakage will collapse.

Brethren, there is a difference between a good idea and God's idea. The power of the bag with holes may give you good ideas but they are not from God. You will keep embracing the good idea but you will refuse to take any godly idea. The spirit will make you to do a correct thing but not the right thing. It will make you do logical things but not the right things.

Sin is the parent of all evils. All manner of evils draw their bitterness from the fountain of sin. Sin is more dangerous than sickness, trials and temptations. Sin is more dangerous than death. Satan cannot overcome you unless he is given authority through sin. Unfortunately, the enemy shields the horrible consequences of sin from you. Every besetting sin will lead to spiritual leakage. You cannot commit sin and say you want to pray for anointing. You cannot be living a sinful life and expect the power of God to remain in your life.

THE POWER OF SIN

You need to deal with sin. If you do not deal with these terrible powers, they will put a powerful evil yoke on your life. You will begin to struggle with satanic yokes and you will not understand why the yokes are so strong. You need to deal with the power of sin in your life. If you don't deal with the bag with holes, you will keep losing your miracles. The spirit of struggling fruitlessly will come upon you. Your life becomes empty. You may pray and receive deliverance but because the bag with holes is attached to your life the deliverance will slip away.

The enemy is able to hang the bag with holes over your neck because of sin. The first act of sin is always very sweet. The waters of sin may be sweet but the consequences are disastrous.

You need to undergo spiritual surgery and break the bag with holes attached to your life. You need to pray that any power causing you to lose your blessings should die. The Bible says, "Touch not my anointed and do my prophet no harm." So you need to cry to the Lord that any evil power touching your blessings should die. You need to pray against anything that makes the blessings of your life to leak away. Pray against any power that is hindering the move of the Holy Spirit in your life. Pray that God should reveal to you the problems of your life, so that you can deal with them.

A man with the spirit of a bag with holes is a frustrated man. You need to deal with it. You need to look into your confidential files if you want the bag with holes to be burnt with fire.

BLOCKING LEAKAGES
A woman came for prayer many years ago, prayed, received blessings and was also delivered. Later, all she got was lost and she came for prayers again. When I started to pray for her, the Lord revealed to me that I should not continue, that she was an evil supervisor and I asked the woman about her being an evil supervisor and she claimed ignorance. I told her to pray about it that God would reveal things to her. After some time she later remembered that when her son got married, she never wanted any woman to take her son away from her so she moved in with this couple into their one-room apartment to inconvenience the wife. As a result of this, she invited the spirit of the bag with

holes into her life, which was then troubling her.

Many christians do a lot of terrible things and keep quiet, thinking that God does not see them. Yes, God sees and forgives them but the consequences of the bag with holes remains. You need to cry to God to deliver you.

You may wonder why things are so difficult for you, why you have to pray very hard before you can get something. It is because the blessings you receive are lost through the bag with holes. You need to repent of your breaking promises, critical spirit, dishonesty, gossip, bearing grudges, keeping malice, envy, lying and greed. If you repent of all these then you have dealt with the spirit of a bag with holes.

You need to deal with procrastination, sex outside marriage, stealing, talkativeness, unbelief and worry, so that you can be delivered from the spirit of the bag with holes. If the entire blessings you have received from God have remained in your life without any leakage, your story would have changed.

Prayer Points

1. My father, restore me today, in the name of Jesus.

2. I receive power to rewrite my family history for

good, in the name of Jesus.

3. Ever power that wants to stop my destiny, I stop you before you stop me, in the name of Jesus.

4. Bag with holes of my father's house, catch fire, in the name of Jesus.

5. Power of praying without result, die, in the name of Jesus.

6. The power of leakage assigned to my life, your time is up. Die, in the name of Jesus.

7. Every blessing that leakage has stolen from me, hear the word of the Lord. Come back, in the name of Jesus.

8. Every power firing arrows at the edge of my breakthroughs, Die, in the name of Jesus.

The Mystery Of First Fruit Offering

1. Be Prepared
2. Breakthrough Prayers For Business Professionals
3. Brokenness
4. Born Great, But Tied Down
5. Can God Trust You?
6. Criminals In The House of God
7. Contending For The Kingdom
8. Dealing With Local Satanic Technology
9. Dealing With Witchcraft Barbers
10. Dealing With Hidden Curses
11. Dealing With The Evil Powers of Your Father's House
12. Dealing With Unprofitable Roots
13. Deliverance: God's Medicine Bottle
14. Deliverance By Fire
15. Deliverance From Spirit Husband And Spirit Wife
16. Deliverance of The Conscience
17. Deliverance of The Head
18. Destiny Clinic
19. Destroying The Evil Umbrella
20. Drawers of Power From The Heavenlies
21. Dominion Prosperity
22. Evil Appetite
23. Facing Both Ways
24. Family Deliverance
25. Fasting And Prayer
26. Failure In The School Of Prayer
27. Freedom From The Grip of Witchcraft
28. From Adversity To Testimony
29. For We Wrestle . . .
30. Holy Cry
31. Holy Fever

ALL OBTAINABLE AT:

Online at www.mountainoffire.org/mfmonlinesales.htm

MFM International Bookshop, 13, Olasimbo Street, Onike, Yaba, Lagos.

IPFY Music Konnections Limited, 48, Opebi Road, Salvation Bus Stop (234–1-4719471, 234-8033056093)

All MFM Church branches nationwide and Christian bookstores.